Charles Kell

Pierre Mask

SV

SurVision Books

First published in 2021 by
SurVision Books
Dublin, Ireland
Reggio di Calabria, Italy
www.survisionmagazine.com

Copyright © Charles Kell, 2021

Cover image: Egon Schiele, *Selbstbildnis, Kopf* (*Self Portrait, Head*), 1910. Private Collection / Photo © Christie's Images / Bridgeman Images

Design © SurVision Books, 2021

ISBN: 978-1-912963-19-5

This book is in copyright. No part of this publication may be reproduced, stored in a retrieval system, or transmitted in any form or by any means without the prior permission in writing from the publisher.

Acknowledgements

Grateful acknowledgement is made to the editors of the following, in which some of these poems, or versions of them, originally appeared:

Abstract; Bluestem; Brooklyn Review; Coffin Bell; Dash; Laurel Review; Layman's Way; MAYDAY; Quiddity; Miracle Monocle; SurVision; Temenos; Treehouse; Up North Lit

Notes: quotes are from Herman Melville's *Moby-Dick; or, The Whale* (1851), *Pierre; or The Ambiguities* (1852), "Bartleby, the Scrivener: A Story of Wall-Street" (1853). "Chronometricals & Horologicals" is from Book XIV, "The Journey of the Pamphlet," of *Pierre*, and from David Faflik's *Melville and the Question of Meaning* (2018). "Pierre's Severed Head" includes lines from Heraclitus, *Fragments* (trans. Brooks Haxton, 2001).

I owe a debt to Steve Langan and his magical first book, *Freezing* (2001), for helping me through a tough time in 2017.

My deep thanks and gratitude to Miguel Murphy for his time, feedback, and friendship.

Contents

Asp	6
The Green Hat	7
Monsieur Melville	8
Pierre the Optimist	9
The Green Hat, Day 2	10
Found Letter	11
The Green Hat, Evening, Day 3	12
Bartleby	13
Dead Letter Office	14
Queequeg Mask	15
Ambergris	16
Pierre in the Field	17
The Green Hat, Day 4	18
Ohio	19
Poetry	20
Egon Schiele's Hideous Phantom	21
The Green Hat, Day 5	22
Pierre the Philosopher	23
Chronometricals & Horologicals	24
Fantastic Fish Mask	25
Melville with a Beard of Snakes	26
The Green Hat, Evening, Day 6	27
Dead Letter Office	28
My Broken Tooth	29
Bartleby Mask	30
Pierre the Pessimist	31
The Green Hat, Day 7	32
Pierre's Severed Head	33
Carrie	34
Ishmael Mask	35

By vast pains we mine into the pyramid; by horrible gropings we come to the central room; with joy we espy the sarcophagus; but we lift the lid—and no body is there!—appallingly vacant as vast is the soul of a man!

—Herman Melville, *Pierre; or, The Ambiguities*

Asp

Feel my shape—fossil
back from black ash

to a picture on the mantel.
Out of that zinc sheet

into a hot bubble. Out of steel
steps dripping white

paint, green skin tossed
off along the rail. Out of names,

nickel, ampersand. The marriage
of tongue to salt back to chilled

aluminum. You were catching
my breath for hours on end.

The Green Hat

lies buried in slush,
alone, stranded on the side
of the street. It wasn't there
yesterday when snow
fell in blurred clumps.

It's large, yet lost children
sometimes wear grown-
up skin when they want
to act somber,
to take on the world's debt.

Someone is waking from
a dream, *where is my green hat?*
A face in a dark room,
another hangover, eyes
burnt eel-black.

Monsieur Melville

Make a fist of smoke then bray
at the stars. November is a paper wing.
Obelisk out of moving water,
on the quay a dangling spur.

All right, sir, are your papers in order?
Is it a nag or a whaler?
With legs like yours, sir, it would
be a sin to go for just a walk.

You are a machine. Your gaze
goes beyond the ball.
Two hundred pounds of sullen
flesh, fifty of corrosive muscle

mast-tied during a storm? Stripped
& lashed with a bullwhip? The truths
insular, viscous. Ants bore into
the planks of the hull, brown flakes

dapple white paper. Ink-smudged.
Call him the guilty one—sparrows
in his eyes. The whole world right
where you stand, there isn't another.

Pierre the Optimist

Alone like a glass violin.
So what, one is never free.

My friends are well for the moment,
they count on the head of a pin.

Collect green grass clippings from
a freshly covered grave.

Hold a gray rock, as waves
soak my leather.

My music box is always open.
Come, the earth is on fire and I am skipping

to a cantata with hints
of cliff's edge, broken bridge—

The Green Hat, Day 2

The Sun hits the green
hat at a sharp right angle
making shadows touch the storm
drain. It's below freezing.
My windows steam.

Someone wears a hat like
that if headed to take
care of serious business.
There are papers that need
signed, yet we wait,

the spirit of godly gamesomeness
is not in ye. God keep me from ever
completing anything. This whole
book is but a draught—nay,
but the draught of a draught

Found Letter

The name look-
ed familiar, blotted
out by a faint
smear. Rain. I stand
in the water,
the moving river,
silver air. Hold
it there.

The Green Hat, Evening, Day 3

The TV is low, we hear
muffled voices
whisper an important secret
just out of reach. I write
two notes about the green hat.

The first describes its texture:
sodden, thick, then frozen,
slush damp, snowy. Skin
cell, probably hard
blonde hairs trapped inside.

The owner must have green
eyes, a body that moves
in confident strides across ice
floes, oceans. A head held
high, one who never looks back—

Bartleby

Look at you with head held high,
the heft of a mountain in a keyhole.

What will your hands be after summer,

after the rain bleeds through?
I prefer not to.

You can teach water to talk this way,

to copy names into a thick blue book.
Stare at a wall like a coffin

falling from a window in the city.

In the office breath hovers over gray
steps, lemony ink.

See one walking with bent back.

On the cloudy ledger, flecks of torn skin.
See him chewing his watch like a leaf—

Dead Letter Office

I wake in the cemetery,
raise my finger
to the foggy sky & draw
a slanted mausoleum.

Place what's left of my
father's ashes inside its mauve
walls. Prop the door with mother's
wooden leg. Carve a window

in the granite so my last
phantom has air.
Each suicide a successful
attempt at sublimation,

the gravedigger warned me.
I am crawling naked
in circles on a mountain
of femur-shaped spirea.

This is what the Bible
promised. I am.
A beetle fingers & toes
flail in the wind.

Queequeg Mask

In the shed, mix creosote & cumin.
Spread its thick paste across my forehead.

Light three sticks of jasmine
& inhale cords of smoke

as the tympanum rattles my skull.
Carve this coffin from oak.

Each night outside of time I stack
the letters on thin strips of glass.

Lie inside its contours, still,
waiting for the wind.

Listen to the harpoon's rattle begin.
If a man made up his mind to live,

mere sickness could not kill him.
Make a life-buoy of the coffin, and no more.

Ambergris

Here, underwater, bubbles are bells.
Whales are cathedrals
who spin in coruscating kelp
while we mimic the ribs of divers,
this one paper lantern
barreling toward
the bottom of the sea.

I chew tinfoil.
Here, in Bruges, bells
are soaked in salty brine.
I kill time.
Tiresias counts important green pebbles.
See my scabs shine
behind foil-wrapped oleander.

Pierre in the Field

How our sleeves trail wet grass.
We hoe corn, we grow wheat.
We collect tart berries in a bucket.

My adversary catches a hand down
my pants—I laugh until tears sing a circle of salt.
We cut tobacco, we heat iron.

My obliques bulge from heavy lifting.
In winter I wear the battered yoke & run
as buckets overflow with thick red paste.

Master wears a hat of furry horns.
We stock the apothecary, we boil onions.
Master slips a finger inside until my

teeth click. The wood is alive with locusts
who smoke & wheeze in the apoplectic dusk.

The Green Hat, Day 4

The fat black grackles
from the cemetery hover
over the green hat. They seem
wary to land, inspect.
I can't say I blame them.

In the town's restaurant, once,
I saw a figure wearing
a green hat not unlike the one
in salt and debris
on the street. I thought

this person knows a thing
about culture. I wiped my hands
on the cloth napkin, ran them
through my thick, brown hair, *now
I know how it feels to be buried.*

Ohio

Drinking Wild Turkey in a peeling
canoe, land-bound, by

the drained swimming pool.

The leaves stare as we turn
to run. Our plan is to break

the glass, swipe the fancy heirloom.

You talk me down with a shy
glance. Later, we huddle in

the flooded basement, watching

the washing machine float by.
We call it a chapel.

Then the rain. Then the snow.

The click-beetles scratching at the door.
Bills in a pile by the gas stove.

I taste your dirty wine scarf; over and full,

your hands knead my stiff neck.
The snow buries the house till we can't see.

Twice I fix soup you refuse to eat.

Poetry

Charles Kell, in his cell.
On rusty springs, staring
through a square window at a distant tree,
dreaming of the wine-dark sea.
He should be taken
behind the fence & beaten.
His leger hand, chop
& stow it so students
can study it as they do pig fetuses
in formaldehyde, the monster
should move no more. He wants
to be a tree. Pumpkinhead
patched with moss, a pile of dust.
Charles Kell, kill yourself.

Egon Schiele's Hideous Phantom

He is a champagne cork shat by the devil.
Star drop of semen in the jagged
    weft
of a broken glass bottle. To push,
to lay, to beat the chest's hair
into matted lumps.
To crumble wet clay into small pellets
that dash in crooks of the wooden
    floor.
Better to burn. To drink rubber liquid
until your hot head blows cold.
Better to pull purple vines
from the rotting trellis. The Inquisitor
waits, brush hangs on the easel's
    scaffold.
Face glistens like larva, halo
of white heat. Sculptor,
carve a lost year into a flame
eating paper. Rat nibbling
an ankle as the robe's knot frays.
These arms are cylinders. Stand
so close insufflate the fine dust.

The Green Hat, Day 5

My erection presses our frosted
windowpane. The wind
outside is fierce yet the green hat
holds ground. You come from
behind, shape your body

to my back. *I'll be right
there,* I breathe. *And we will
drive holes into our centers
where words can no longer
fit.* You laugh, grow quiet.

The plants need water, the house
settles. As I turn to descend
the green hat flickers. No,
it was the last lamp
on the street burning out—

Pierre the Philosopher

Soft cloth stretches to Santa Fe.
The mountain is window,
linseed oil.
In a forest off the high-
way thousands of gray
mushrooms grow unfettered.
The Unfettered Finn is what we
once called him.

Now, let it soak.
Cake your fingernails in wax.
Let the circular motion act
as impediment, antidepressant.
Relax. What a quiet stampede.
What a soft way to end a parade.
A train floats over the tracks.

It is raining mushrooms, monsieur.
Her long hair arbored him in ebon vines.

Chronometricals & Horologicals

A lesson which Pierre would appear
to be receptive. *In things terrestrial,
a man must not be governed
by ideas celestial.*

We never learn. No conclusion
of what remains. A map, gambit.
The pamphlet offers a false dichotomy.
The effort to live in this world

*is, somehow, apt to invoke
those inferior beings in strange, unique
follies and sins, unimagined before.*
He walks away still clinging

to an *infallible instinct.* April.
Apathy. A deeply felt unfeeling.
Here the pages are torn,
and come to a not untidy termination.

Fantastic Fish Mask

with eyes on each side. One
gazes toward the grim
mountain while the other stares
low at a blood-flecked pearl.
You can still smoke a cigar
& not get sick,
pull a sip from this Knob
Creek, whistle a sea
ditty. You have windows for pockets.
Gaze at the five-dollar bill
gripped with damp blue fuzz.
Spooled cassette tape salted with brine.
You walk along the lake,
open your mouth into a cosmic O.
Yes, that's a tail
you burly one, you can't lick.
You're not air. Those circles
are brushing your scales, slick fin.

Melville with a Beard of Snakes

Sandpaper tongue, Mephistopheles.
Quiver of a saw in wind,
on your knees naked in the mangroves,
perforated with nails.

He is a robber on the run
aloft in a galleon
floating on a whitecap over
the Indian Ocean. Felon.

Loose Virginia tobacco
rolled into a delicate pin.
Smoke floats, a curtain of bees.
There is no pier, no shelter.

No bottom, destination.
Water never ends. There is no
Boston. In a locked room. I have eaten
Jules Verne & turned into a loom.

The Green Hat, Evening, Day 6

In the film version of Michael
Arlen's melodramatic
novel, *The Green Hat,*
Greta Garbo plays Iris Storm,
a woman of "unsavory

reputation," whose first
husband commits suicide on
their wedding night. I wish
for a cigar to smoke, a touch
of whiskey, as I stand, thinking

about the viridian. Yellow
gripped curling edges
of worn books. A cactus
knowing water. Chairs
afloat in an ocean of trees.

Dead Letter Office

Work papers bound in blue string;
ink covers the table, runs over

a slanted floor; keyholes rattle in a cold New
Bedford wind. Here, in my mouth again.

Sweating barrel of an empty bottle.
Phlegm from a November catarrh.

This is the *Etching of Plague Years.*
Barbed wire, tourmaline, lye soap.

The sister text that began with
The Book of Salt, Sand & Rope.

A fly spins on a sheet of white melamine.
A fly is frozen in a glim of ice.

My Broken Tooth

The night my father died the Winter
Olympics blared from
the floating TV. They skied down
through the closed-captioned snow.
My father looked screwed, a spare
tire under the double bed.
A purple marble like a giant eye
floating above his head.
I cracked it on glass, he said.
His Ahab tattoo frowned under a dim lamp.
Chalk in a cheek to pump down the shaky jaw.
The drinker's face repeats.
Somewhere in Nagano a neon sign blinks
making the faux fur gleam.

Bartleby Mask

No plot, no narrative, a wanderer
who refuses to budge.
Karl Marx in cement covered in silver mollusks.
Air forces a low hum
from the throat.
I know where I am.
If the prisoner tries to sleep throw water on him.
Or hit him with bamboo sticks.
Shine florescent light into the whites of his eyes.
Slash his letter to pieces until
the medicine kicks in. Cadaverous causality.
Behold my face from locust exuviae,
terminalia, glass pieces burnt green,
baptized by the sudden shock of a light socket.

Pierre the Pessimist

What is a tale told by an idiot called?
His hands now tickle the harp,

watching with measured alacrity
while the world dissolves.

My little instrument is broken again,
dripping with treatment,

in search of lost time as the tired nurse
ties another bandage.

What do the stairwells on top of stairwells mean?
I feel lean in the jowl, with a hungry look.

A beetle, almost, pink foam pearls for eyes.
I rip the book, douse each page with gasoline.

My strings. They peel the skin-of-my-teeth
down to the quick. Please, doctor, fix it.

The Green Hat, Day 7

A rat runs in small
circles where the green
hat used to lie. A stranger
with heavy hands must
have snatched it walking by.

My eyelids feel dipped
in sand. The knocking of
the shutter shakes our white
walls. A painting falls. A door
slams. Shelves tilt like a galleon's

hull, spilling knick-knacks
over the wine-stained carpet.
Sleep, the confession
is half over. Even the judge
is weary. Nails rain down, crack

the window. The green hat

somewhere in a coal-veined sky.

Pierre's Severed Head

stares at the light blinking blue
from frozen branches.
A wonder it still hungers and wants
after such a long separation—
propped on this abandoned roll top desk,
stuck with black moss,
in the middle of a forgotten wood.

I talk and talk—a babble of violet.
O iron and umber
O Great Aluminum Reef.

Dab its damp brow with a cotton swab.
Stick a bent straw between chapped lips.
Whisper Heraclitus: *After death comes*
nothing hoped for nor imagined.

I pack tepid clay softly in its ears to protect
    it from the piercing cry.

There is a pyramid on the other side
where the head (some say) might be considered
a god.

The judas-hole, the inmate, the marrow glowing like

Carrie

I'm a yellow balloon filled with
blood tethered to your acrylic easel,
like I'm back, age thirteen,
   sniffing glue
in the middle school basement,
both of us waiting for the future,
knowing we would meet
  and end up
here, which isn't true—it was an accident,
luck—I want to draw you, sitting
on our couch,
in your pink robe, legs
slightly open, gazing at the TV, my body
at last grounded, a book of French poetry
open on the coffee table;
I've been
drawing you all this time,
  as I hover
in the atmosphere, drunk on thin air,
ready to burst, the brown strands
of your hair keeping me
attached to this world,
and I promise
you as I've promised you for ten years,

I will never float
away, don't let me float away

Ishmael Mask

I am homeless. The ocean is my home.

More poetry published by SurVision Books

Noelle Kocot. *Humanity*
(New Poetics: USA)
ISBN 978-1-9995903-0-7

Ciaran O'Driscoll. *The Speaking Trees*
(New Poetics: Ireland)
ISBN 978-1-9995903-1-4

Helen Ivory. *Maps of the Abandoned City*
(New Poetics: England)
ISBN 978-1-912963-04-1

Elin O'Hara Slavick. *Cameramouth*
(New Poetics: USA)
ISBN 978-1-9995903-4-5

John W. Sexton. *Inverted Night*
(New Poetics: Ireland)
ISBN 978-1-912963-05-8

Afric McGlinchey. *Invisible Insane*
(New Poetics: Ireland)
ISBN 978-1-9995903-3-8

Anatoly Kudryavitsky. *Stowaway*
(New Poetics: Ireland)
ISBN 978-1-9995903-2-1

Tim Murphy. *The Cacti Do Not Move*
(New Poetics: Ireland)
ISBN 978-1-912963-07-2

Tony Kitt. *The Magic Phlute*
(New Poetics: Ireland)
ISBN 978-1-912963-08-9

Clayre Benzadón. *Liminal Zenith*
(New Poetics: USA)
ISBN 978-1-912963-11-9

Thomas Townsley. *Tangent of Ardency*
(New Poetics: USA)
ISBN 978-1-912963-15-7

Matthew Geden. *Fruit*
(New Poetics: Ireland)
ISBN 978-1-912963-16-4

Marc Vincenz. *Einstein Fledermaus*
(New Poetics: USA)
ISBN 978-1-912963-20-1

George Kalamaras. *That Moment of Wept*
ISBN 978-1-9995903-7-6

Anton Yakovlev. *Chronos Dines Alone*
(Winner of James Tate Poetry Prize 2018)
ISBN 978-1-912963-01-0

Bob Lucky. *Conversation Starters in a Language No One Speaks*
(Winner of James Tate Poetry Prize 2018)
ISBN 978-1-912963-00-3

Christopher Prewitt. *Paradise Hammer*
(Winner of James Tate Poetry Prize 2018)
ISBN 978-1-9995903-9-0

Mikko Harvey & Jake Bauer. *Idaho Falls*
(Winner of James Tate Poetry Prize 2018)
ISBN 978-1-912963-02-7

Tony Bailie. *Mountain Under Heaven*
(Winner of James Tate Poetry Prize 2019)
ISBN 978-1-912963-09-6

Nicholas Alexander Hayes. *Amorphous Organics*
(Winner of James Tate Poetry Prize 2019)
ISBN 978-1-912963-10-2

John Bradley. *Spontaneous Mummification*
(Winner of James Tate Poetry Prize 2019)
ISBN 978-1-912963-13-3

John Thomas Allen. *Rolling in the Third Eye*
(Winner of James Tate Poetry Prize 2019)
ISBN 978-1-912963-15-7

Gary Glauber. *The Covalence of Equanimity*
(Winner of James Tate Poetry Prize 2019)
ISBN 978-1-912963-12-6

Maria Grazia Calandrone. *Fossils*
Translated from Italian
(New Poetics: Italy)
ISBN 978-1-9995903-6-9

Sergey Biryukov. *Transformations*
Translated from Russian
(New Poetics: Russia)
ISBN 978-1-9995903-5-2

Alexander Korotko. *Irrazionalismo*
Translated from Russian
(New Poetics: Ukraine)
ISBN 978-1-912963-06-5

Anton G. Leitner. *Selected Poems 1981–2015*
Translated from German
ISBN 978-1-9995903-8-3

message-door: An Anthology of Contemporary Surrealist Poetry from Russia (bilingual)
Edited and translated from Russian by Anatoly Kudryavitsky
ISBN 978-1-912963-17-1

Seeds of Gravity: An Anthology of Contemporary Surrealist Poetry from Ireland
Edited by Anatoly Kudryavitsky
ISBN 978-1-912963-18-8

All our books are available to order via
http://survisionmagazine.com/books.htm

www.ingramcontent.com/pod-product-compliance
Lightning Source LLC
Chambersburg PA
CBHW061313040426
42444CB00010B/2611